This book is to be returned on or before
the last date stamped below.

IRAQ

Simon Ponsford

W

FRANKLIN WATTS

LONDON•SYDNEY

Designer Rita Storey
Editor Sarah Ridley
Art Director Jonathan Hair
Editor-in-Chief John C. Miles
Picture research Diana Morris

First published in 2006 by Franklin Watts

Franklin Watts
338 Euston Road
London NW1 3BH

Franklin Watts Australia
Hachette Children's Books
Level 17/207 Kent Street
Sydney NSW 2000

A CIP catalogue record for this book
is available from the British Library.

Dewey classification number: 915.67

ISBN 978 0 7496 6431 2

Printed in China

Franklin Watts is a division of Hachette Children's Books.

CONTENTS

1   Geography and People   4

2   A Short History   6

3   People of Iraq: Sunnis and Shia   8

4   People of Iraq: The Kurds   10

5   Saddam Hussein: His Rise and Fall   12

6   Iraq's Oil Industry   14

7   Key Moments: War with Iran   16

8   Key Moments: Saddam Takes on the West   18

9   Everyday Struggles   20

10 Children in Iraq   22

11 Women in Iraq   24

12 Iraq: What's in Store?   26

13 Timeline + Basic Facts   28

14 Glossary and Websites 30

15 Index 32

1 GEOGRAPHY AND PEOPLE

ON THE EASTERN EDGE OF THE MIDDLE EAST LIES IRAQ, *a land with a rich and turbulent history. Almost 60 per cent of Iraq is desert (where "even a desert snake would feel lonely", as one geography textbook puts it). Yet there are snow-clad mountains in the north, and fertile marshes in the south.*

Two huge rivers, the Tigris and the Euphrates, are the lifeblood of Iraq. They flow down from the north and meet in southern Iraq, creating farmland along the river banks. The two rivers then form the Shatt al-Arab waterway, which flows into the Persian or Arabian Gulf.

Iraq has a population of 26 million and is about the size of France. It is almost land-locked, with only a tiny stretch of

GROUNDS FOR DEBATE

Iraq makes a lot of money from selling oil to other countries. It comes from oilfields in the north and south, and some people there think the oil income should only benefit their areas. But people in the middle of Iraq say that would be wrong. They think the central government in Baghdad should continue to share out the money fairly across the country.

coastline. No less than six countries share its borders: Iran, Turkey, Syria, Jordan, Saudi Arabia and Kuwait.

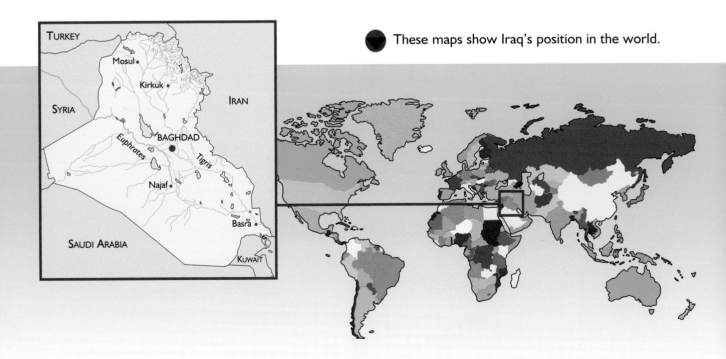

These maps show Iraq's position in the world.

PEOPLES

The main religion in Iraq is Islam, and 80 per cent of people are Arab. As well as the Arab Muslim majority, Iraq has several minority groups. Of these, the Kurds are the biggest group and play a key role.

Iraq is divided into 18 provinces, each with its own governor. Central government is based in the ancient city of Baghdad, the capital. There are famous holy shrines in towns such as Najaf. Other important places include Mosul and Kirkuk in the north, and the city of Basra in the south. Both areas are rich in oil, which is vital to the economy.

FARMING AND DAILY LIFE

Apart from oil, Iraq does not export a great variety of products. It does sell a large amount of dates abroad, since it has about 22 million date trees. Otherwise, people grow wheat and barley in the north-west, and there are rice fields in the south. Farming can be difficult as floods occur regularly.

Most Iraqis now live in towns and cities, but in some rural and mountainous areas people still live tribal or even nomadic lives. The family and tribal identity are very important to all Iraqis, who are often described as a warm and generous people.

Iraq has been in the worldwide news since 1979 when President Saddam Hussein took charge. Since the invasion by US-led forces in 2003, Iraq has struggled to rebuild itself.

KNOW YOUR FACTS

At least 95 per cent of Iraq's people are Muslims. The majority are Shia Muslims, who follow a version of the faith known as Shi'ism. Traditionally, though, Iraq's political rulers, including Saddam Hussein, have come from among the minority Sunni Muslims. Since Saddam lost power in 2003, the Shia and Sunnis have been trying to reach agreement on how to share power and resources in Iraq.

The northern part of Iraq is mountainous.

MODERN IRAQ STANDS ON LAND THAT WAS ONCE PART OF MESOPOTAMIA, *an area historians call the "cradle of civilisation". This is because, in about 3000BCE, many important features of modern-day life and culture began to take root there: from farming to writing, from legal systems to architecture.*

Many of those early discoveries still echo down the ages. The zero was introduced into mathematics, as was the system of dividing an hour into 60 minutes and 60 seconds. An early code of law was established and Mesopotamia had some of the earliest examples of the wheel and of writing.

However, Mesopotamia was also a land of war. People fought each other to defend and expand their territories around the two great rivers, the Tigris and the Euphrates. Different civilisations flourished in turn: Sumerian, Akkadian, Assyrian and Babylonian.

 Islam has played a key part in Iraq's history. This is the shrine of Imam Ali al Naqi and Imam al Askari in the town of Samarra.

Empires came and went. Persia – today's Iran – took control in 550BCE but lost out to Alexander the Great of Greece two hundred years later. And so the battle for Mesopotamia went on until the 7th century CE, when Islam began.

ISLAM ARRIVES

Islam was based on the teachings of the Prophet Muhammad, and its followers had a profound influence on the world. Under the Abbasid dynasty, Islam united many peoples and countries, spreading from Spain in the west, to India in the east.

In 762, Baghdad became the capital of the Muslim world. At the time, it was the most advanced civilisation in the world, leading the way in art, literature, science, medicine, architecture and commerce.

All that came to a brutal end in the 13th century when the Mongol army from Central Asia reached Baghdad. They destroyed the city, killing three-quarters of a million people, burning books and throwing them in the river. Today, little is left of ancient Baghdad.

After the Mongols, Persian and Turkish rulers competed to bring the area into their empires. In the 18th and 19th centuries, the Ottoman Turks – the superpower of their day – were in control. But other European countries had their eye on the area. Britain, for example, wanted unbroken shipping links with part of its empire, India.

BRITISH OCCUPATION

The British Army occupied the area during World War One (1914-18). When the war was over, three Ottoman provinces were joined together and became modern-day Iraq. Britain remained in control of the region until it was thought to be ready for independence.

Britain put a pro-British king in power and in 1932 Iraq became an independent country, at least in name. But there was coup after coup, and in 1958 army officers successfully overthrew the king and Iraq became a republic.

Ten years after that, Saddam Hussein's Ba'ath party took power by force and Saddam became president in 1979. He ruled with an iron fist until US-led troops invaded in 2003.

GROUNDS FOR DEBATE

Relics from ancient times help us to understand Iraq's history. Sadly, after the US-led invasion in 2003, many were damaged or destroyed. Looters broke into the museum in Baghdad, stealing more than 15,000 priceless objects. Many are still missing. Some people argue that it could not have been avoided, because of the chaos of war. Others, such as archaeologists, think it is a crime against history and that the US Army should have done more to prevent it.

3 PEOPLE OF IRAQ: SUNNIS AND SHIA

THE SEEDS OF MANY OF THE PROBLEMS *facing today's Iraq were planted a long time ago, and the roots are deep. In the case of the Sunni and Shia Muslims, the divisions go back to the 7th century.*

After the death of the Prophet Muhammad in 632, there was a dispute over who should follow him as the new leader of Islam. Some Muslims (now known as the Sunni) thought it should be one of his closest followers. Others (now the Shia) believed Muhammad's son-in-law Ali and his descendants should lead the Muslims. After a series of battles, they broke into two groups, or sects. Centuries later, they are still divided.

The Sunnis form the vast majority of Muslims across the world – about 90 per cent. In Iraq, though, they are the minority. In spite of this, it is the Sunnis, not the Shia, who have traditionally held the important jobs in Iraq.

Saddam Hussein is a Sunni, and during his rule he took that domination to new levels. He oppressed and persecuted all his opponents, to try to extinguish any threat to his rule. The Shia were often his target.

Friday prayers at the Imam al Kadhim shrine in Baghdad.

A Marsh Arab glides past a traditional reed house.

BRUTAL REPRESSION

The most vicious attacks came after the First Gulf War in 1991. The Shia in the south rebelled against Saddam, believing that US forces would support them. They did not. On Saddam's orders, thousands of Shia were killed by Iraqi troops.

Saddam also took revenge on a unique Shia community, the Marsh Arabs. He accused them of protecting his enemies. As punishment, the Marsh Arabs were attacked and their marshlands were drained. Thousands had to flee; about 20 per cent of them died.

Since Saddam Hussein lost power in 2003, the Shia and the Sunnis have struggled to agree on the direction Iraq should take, and there has been an explosion of violence. The Shia

KNOW YOUR FACTS

In the 1990s, when Saddam Hussein used dams to drain water from the area where the Marsh Arabs live, he wiped out their rare and ancient way of life. For 5,000 years the Marsh Arabs' home was among the reed beds fed by the Tigris and Euphrates rivers. Out of those reeds, they built their traditional round-roofed homes raised on mud banks above the water. They farmed using water buffalo, and fished as well. There have been attempts to flood the marshes again but the worry is that the ecosystem may be damaged beyond repair.

community has been the target of a bombing campaign led by Sunni militants. Many people have been killed and injured.

Moderate leaders on both sides have called for tolerance, and most people want to live together peacefully. But tensions are high and there are warnings that the conflict could end in civil war

THE KURDS ARE THE LARGEST GROUP *of people in the world seeking their own independent country. In all, there are 25 million of them scattered through a region that includes Iraq, Turkey, Syria, Iran and Armenia.*

In Iraq, 20 per cent of the population (about five million people) are Kurdish. Most live in the mountainous north, with its splendid snowy peaks. They are mainly Sunni Muslims, like Saddam Hussein himself, but not Arab. They have their

The bodies of gas victims at Halabjah, 1988.

own culture, history, clothes and language. Like the Shia Muslims, Kurds were oppressed under Saddam's rule and were often persecuted.

In 1988, Saddam led a notorious ethnic-cleansing campaign against the Kurds. He accused the Kurds of helping Iran during the Iran-Iraq War. As a result, Iraqi troops destroyed hundreds of villages and used chemical weapons to kill Kurds, most infamously in the town of Halabjah.

In 1991, in the aftermath of the First Gulf War, the Kurds rose up against Saddam Hussein, expecting US support. When this did not arrive, Iraqi forces crushed the Kurdish rebellion. This left many dead and one-and-a-half million Kurds fled for their lives to other countries.

KNOW YOUR FACTS

The name of a northern Kurdish town, Halabjah, symbolises Saddam Hussein's vicious crackdown on the Kurds. During the Iran-Iraq War in the 1980s, some Kurdish fighters helped Iran. Saddam was outraged at what he saw as gross disloyalty to the nation of Iraq, so in 1988 he ordered his soldiers to kill hundreds of ordinary Kurds in Halabjah. They released a colourless poison gas into the air which caused a horribly painful death.

SAFE AT LAST?

To guard them from further attack by Saddam, the international community eventually declared Iraq's Kurdish region a safe haven. Since then, the Kurds have mostly ruled themselves in an area called Kurdistan, but they are still part of Iraq. They share income from oil with the central government in Baghdad.

Kurdistan is gradually becoming more secure and prosperous. But it has been a long and violent journey, and the struggle is far from over.

The prosperous town of Suleimaniya is in Kurdish-controlled northern Iraq.

GROUNDS FOR DEBATE

Does Kurdish autonomy offer a model for Iraq to follow? After the overthrow of Saddam Hussein in 2003, some places in central and southern Iraq became no-go zones, because of bombings and kidnappings by rebels. In Kurdistan, on the other hand, things were looking up. In the regional capital, Irbil, there was a smart new international airport, built on the site of a former military base used by Saddam Hussein to attack the Kurds.

In other Kurdish towns, like Suleimaniya, new buildings were springing up fast and new businesses were moving in. Iraqi Arabs were moving north to find work. And, unlike in other parts of the country, Kurdish families felt safe enough to spend days out among the picturesque mountains, rivers and waterfalls of Kurdistan.

SADDAM HUSSEIN: HIS RISE AND FALL

SADDAM MEANS "ONE WHO CONFRONTS", *and Saddam Hussein has always lived up to his name. He went from being a small-time gangster, to the leader of a country that took on the world's superpowers.*

Saddam Hussein was born in 1937 into a poor family living near the town of Tikrit on the Tigris river. Saddam never knew his father, and his stepfather beat him. At the age of ten, he left home to live with his uncle.

Saddam's political journey began when he joined a political group called the Ba'ath party. The party was angry at the way European powers had controlled Iraq, and believed Arabs should be one nation.

The Ba'ath party took power in a coup, a military uprising, in 1968. Saddam Hussein was made vice-president, but was in charge of the day-to-day running of the country.

GROUNDS FOR DEBATE

Saddam Hussein ruled by fear. But that does not mean everyone was happy when he was toppled. Some people benefited from his rule, because of links to his family. Others say Saddam held the country together for the benefit of his people, and that during his rule they did not suffer the bombings, kidnappings and chaos that plagued people's daily lives after the US-led invasion of 2003.

When he became president in 1979, he sent 500 of his own party to their deaths, accusing them of plotting against him.

Saddam waves to the crowd at his 61st birthday celebrations in 1998.

FACTS ABOUT SADDAM

Like many brutal dictators, Saddam wanted people to love and celebrate him every day of their lives. There were flattering portraits of Saddam everywhere you went, and many songs were specially written for him. They would be played every day before news broadcasts, which would praise him to the skies. He used people who looked like him – Saddam "doubles" – to make it more difficult for would-be assassins. If he did not want to meet someone, he would send his double.

FEAR AND REPRESSION
Saddam was a terrifying ruler who made everyone frightened to disagree with him. His secret police were everywhere. In schools, children had to tell their teachers if their parents said anything bad about Saddam. If the Ba'ath party decided you were a troublemaker, you could end up in jail or even dead.

Saddam used much of the country's oil wealth to buy weapons from other countries like France, Britain, the former Soviet Union and the USA. He also bought the technology to make chemical weapons, which he later used against his own people.

During his reign, there was one crisis after another. He spent all Iraq's money

Behind the smile, Saddam was a ruthless and brutal dictator.

going to war with Iran in 1980 and in trying to take over its oil-rich neighbour Kuwait in 1990. The outside world thought there would be a coup against Saddam Hussein to topple him from power, but he kept his grip until the US-led invasion in 2003.

In December that year Saddam was captured hiding in a hole in the ground near his home town of Tikrit. He had a straggly grey beard and sunken eyes, a shadow of the strongman who had taunted the world. Saddam was later charged with crimes against humanity.

6 IRAQ'S OIL INDUSTRY

OIL HAS SOMETIMES MADE IRAQ VERY RICH, *and helped improve the lives of its people. But it has also been the spark for war, often with disastrous results.*

Iraq first found oil in big quantities in 1927, at Kirkuk in the north of the country. For many years, Iraq had no direct control over its oil as a foreign-owned company had the right to decide what to do with it. That all changed in 1972, when the Iraqi government took over ownership of the oil reserves.

The decision came at a very good time for Iraq. There was a huge rise in world oil prices after the Arab-Israeli War in 1973 which meant that Iraq earned billions of dollars from selling oil abroad.

KNOW YOUR FACTS

Iraq is swimming in oil. It has 112 billion barrels of reserves, second only to Saudi Arabia. Also about 10 per cent of all the oil that we know is left in the world is in Iraq. Iraq produces 1.8 million barrels every day. Most of it is sold abroad. Oil from countries like Iraq is important to many people around the world because without it, cars, homes, offices and industry would all grind to a halt.

Oil is vital to the economy of Iraq. This is the main Iraq/Kuwait pipeline.

Iraq used some of that money to invest in popular projects, like building and transport schemes, better education, health services and social security. However, a big chunk of the revenue from oil was used to buy dangerous weapons from abroad.

DAMAGE AND DEFEAT

Iraq's oil industry was badly damaged during the Iran-Iraq War in the 1980s when pipelines and refineries were blown up. At the same time, the price of oil dropped worldwide. Iraq built up huge debts.

Things got worse when Saddam Hussein ordered an invasion of Kuwait in 1990, hoping to get hold of their oil supplies. An international armed force defeated his troops. As Iraqi forces retreated they set fire to hundreds of oil wells.

OIL FOR FOOD

In the 1990s the Iraqi oil industry was in chaos. Under United Nations sanctions, Iraq was not allowed to sell any oil abroad. Tens of thousands of people are believed to have died as a result of the lack of medical supplies and food that this caused. In 1996, the UN allowed Iraq to sell oil to buy food and medicine.

WHAT DO YOU THINK?

Some people say that oil will be the saviour of Iraq's struggling economy. They believe it will make the country stable again, bring jobs and peace. Others argue that it is because of Iraq's oil resources that powerful countries like the USA and Britain have meddled in Iraq's affairs, and that this has contributed to today's problems. So is oil a blessing or a curse?

Today, after the invasion of 2003, Iraq's oil industry is trying to get back on its feet. The hope is that money from selling oil abroad will be used to give Iraqis a better future.

An oil well blazes in Southern Iraq in 1990.

IRAQ AND IRAN HAVE A LONG HISTORY OF CONFLICT, *going all the way back to the split over who would succeed the Prophet Muhammad. Iraq is part of the Arab world; Iranians are Persian. There have been countless arguments over who owns land or waterways on their borders.*

In September 1980, those simmering tensions exploded. Saddam Hussein sent his tanks into Iran, and began a war that lasted eight years. Up to a million people died in the war which cost about 600 billion US dollars. So why did it happen?

REVOLUTION IN IRAN

One reason was the big political change in Iran in 1979 caused by a revolution. The secular government of the Shah, which was supported by western countries such as the USA, was overthrown. The Islamic leader, Ayatollah Khomeini, took power.

The Ayatollah had lived in exile in Iraq in the 1960s and 70s. He called on Iraqi Shia Muslims to rise up against Saddam Hussein, and criticised Arab nations that had the backing of western countries.

Saddam thought he would be a hero of the Arab world if he stood up to the Iranians. Influential Arab countries like Saudi Arabia gave him their support.

KNOW YOUR FACTS

Iran was very pleased at the overthrow of Saddam Hussein in 2003. It took care of an old enemy, and has given a lot of power to Iraqi Shia politicians who are friendly to Iran. In 2005 the two countries signed new economic and military deals. The Iraqi Prime Minister at the time was Ibrahim Jaafari, who had lived in asylum in Iran for many years. The USA does not like it, but Iran and Iraq are now close allies.

Iraqi forces go to war in 1980.

WAR BEGINS

Saddam began by invading an oil-rich area in the south of Iran. As many Arabs lived there, Saddam thought they would see him as their saviour, and rebel against Iran. They did not. Iran beat back the Iraqi forces, beginning a long and grinding war. Each side would achieve some victories, then be forced to retreat.

Iran and Iraq finally agreed a ceasefire in 1988. Their oil industries were badly damaged and they both had huge debts. Many families had been ripped apart by the war. Iraq claimed victory, but it was more like a defeat for both sides.

GROUNDS FOR DEBATE

One important American, former US Secretary of State Henry Kissinger, famously said it was a pity both sides could not lose the Iran-Iraq War. For western countries, it was about keeping a balance of power in the Middle East on which they depended for their oil supply. They were afraid of Iran becoming more powerful, but they did not like Saddam Hussein much either. So at times the US and others provided weapons to both Iran and Iraq, because it suited them to keep the war going.

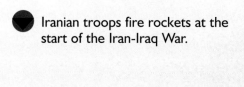

Iranian troops fire rockets at the start of the Iran-Iraq War.

KEY MOMENTS: SADDAM TAKES ON THE WEST

8

AFTER THE WAR WITH IRAN, IRAQ NEEDED TIME TO RECOVER AND REBUILD. *Instead, Saddam Hussein chose to catapult his troops into another battle – the battle for Kuwait.*

Saddam ordered the invasion of Kuwait in August 1990, saying that Kuwait and its oil belonged to Iraq. The international community, and even Arab nations who usually supported him, warned him not to go ahead with the invasion.

Iraqi troops took over Kuwait without a struggle. But countries from around the world met at the United Nations and agreed to work together to free Kuwait. Countries that usually supported Saddam voted to fight him.

It was a short but brutal campaign. Most of the damage was done by air strikes, with high-tech military planes. There was widespread damage and some innocent people died because of bombs that landed in the wrong place.

AN INCOMPLETE DEFEAT

The USA and its allies defeated Saddam Hussein in February 1991, but did not remove him from power. They thought that Saddam's enemies within Iraq would do the job for them. There were uprisings against him, but when foreign troops did not support them, Saddam was able to crush his opponents and keep control.

The 1990s were painful for the Iraqi people. The UN ban on selling oil abroad meant that Iraq had no money to rebuild after yet another war.

 British troops in action as an oil well blazes.

BUT WHERE ARE THE WMDs?

At the same time, there was suspicion that Saddam Hussein was still making nuclear, biological and chemical weapons, known as weapons of mass destruction (WMD). But he refused to allow international weapons inspectors to come and see what he had. This led to his downfall.

US President George W Bush decided to take action against Saddam after Al-Qaeda's suicide attacks on the USA on 11 September 2001. Even though Saddam had no links to Al-Qaeda, President Bush argued that the Iraqi president was a threat to US security, and tried to persuade other countries to join an invasion of Iraq. Many disagreed and this time only a small joint force, led by the USA and Britain, went to war.

In March 2003 they began "Operation Iraqi Freedom". The airforces bombed from the air, then the armies invaded on the ground. A month later, Saddam had fled and his regime was finished.

The USA expected Iraqis to be happy to be rid of Saddam but the story was far from over. After the war, some people argued that the United Nations should take charge of Iraq, until Iraqis were ready to rule themselves. But the Americans wanted the lead role. With the help of allies like Britain, they set about trying to restore law and order and basic services, and to guide Iraq on the road to democracy.

In June 2004, the USA chose Iraqi politicians from all ethnic groups to run the country, although some saw that government as just a puppet of the USA. Iraqi people themselves then voted in January and December 2005, to choose new leaders to tackle Iraq's many problems. Because of daily outbreaks of violence, it was a country where guns and bombs seemed to rule, not politicians.

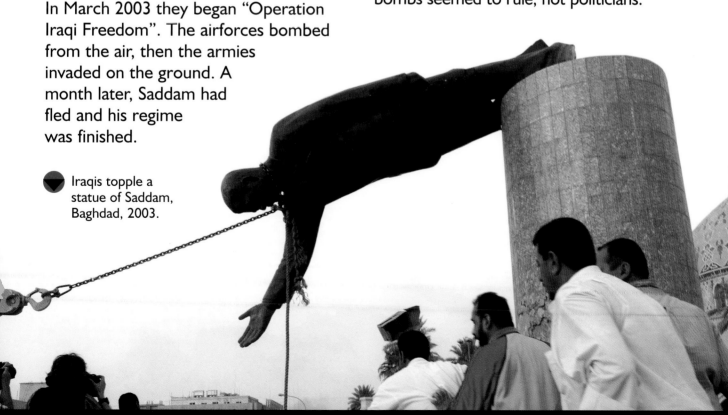

● Iraqis topple a statue of Saddam, Baghdad, 2003.

SINCE SADDAM HUSSEIN LOST POWER, *Iraq has faced a new set of problems. The first is how to rebuild a country shattered by more than 20 years of war and neglect. The second is how to do this while bombers and kidnappers are terrorising many of the people who live there.*

Most of the bombs go off in or around Baghdad, where the Sunni Muslims have their stronghold. The bombers target both foreign troops and ordinary Iraqis, for example people lining up to look for work. In 2005, the bombers even killed several children who were taking sweets from American troops. Many Iraqis also have to deal with kidnappers, who demand thousands of US dollars for the release of family members.

DAILY CHALLENGES

Day-to-day life can be a struggle. Water supplies are often unreliable, and not safe to drink without boiling. Sometimes there are pools of sewage in the street because toilets do not work properly. There are fuel shortages and long queues for petrol, so some people end up buying it at inflated prices on the black market.

Iraqis queueing to collect their oil ration, 2005.

GROUNDS FOR DEBATE

Who are the bombers, and how can they be stopped? They seem to come mainly from two groups: either supporters of Saddam Hussein who are angry at his downfall, or extremist Muslim groups linked to Al-Qaeda, who are fighting jihad or "holy war" against occupying troops. The Iraqi government believes the bombers will lose strength as Iraq's newly trained police and army start taking over from foreign troops. Another way to stop the bombers could be to gain better intelligence on what they are planning. And longer term, the hope is that Iraq will become more wealthy, and the problem will disappear.

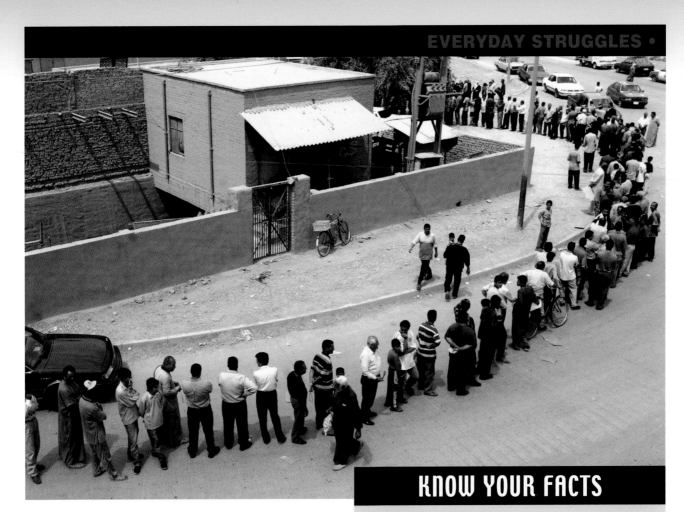

People queue for bread at a bakery in Baghdad.

Electricity is also a key problem. Pipes and cables are easily damaged by people who oppose the foreign troops. The United States is spending about $18 billion on long-term reconstruction projects, but some of that money has had to be diverted to pay for security.

Unemployment is another big issue for Iraq. In 2005, a third or more of people had no job. For those in work, wages were often too low to support a family. Even two years after the US-led invasion, a quarter of Iraqis were still totally dependent on food rations to survive. Some had to sell those rations for other needs, such as medicine.

KNOW YOUR FACTS

Iraq's health system was one of the best in the region in the 1970s but, like many other services, it has collapsed. In 2002, for example, the country spent just $16 million on its people's health: that is less than a dollar per person. Things are improving: in 2004, for example, the budget was up to $1 billion. But Iraq's health services still desperately need repair and rebuilding. They are crying out for new equipment and more medicines. Another problem is that many well-trained doctors are trying to leave the country to work abroad.

HALF OF IRAQ'S POPULATION IS UNDER THE AGE OF 18. *That means most children have known little but war, and their health and education have suffered greatly.*

The United Nations says that before the invasion of Iraq in 2003, one in eight Iraqi children were dying before their fifth birthday. Diseases spread quickly because of dirty water and shortages of medicines, and children were weak from lack of food.

After the war, children's health generally began to improve. But some Iraqi children were still starving and their growth was stunted. Many still had no clean water, and were hit by outbreaks of diarrhoea and respiratory diseases.

A lot of these problems began in the 1990s, when Iraq was under UN sanctions. It is a grim contrast with Iraq in the 1970s, when health officials say life was good, and their problem for the future seemed more likely to be people being over-weight, rather than starving.

BACK TO SCHOOL

Education is also a big issue. A generation ago, Iraq had the best school system in the region. But after the 2003 war, according to the United Nations, millions of Iraqi children had to go to schools with crumbling walls, broken toilets and leaking roofs. Some schools had been bombed, others looted, leaving a shortage of classrooms, desks, chairs and books.

There has been some progress. More teachers are being trained and books distributed. Iraq has plans to rebuild thousands of new schools and colleges. But a year after the fall of Saddam, at least one in five children had no primary education, and about half did not go on to secondary school.

Iraqi children queue to examine a US tank in Baghdad.

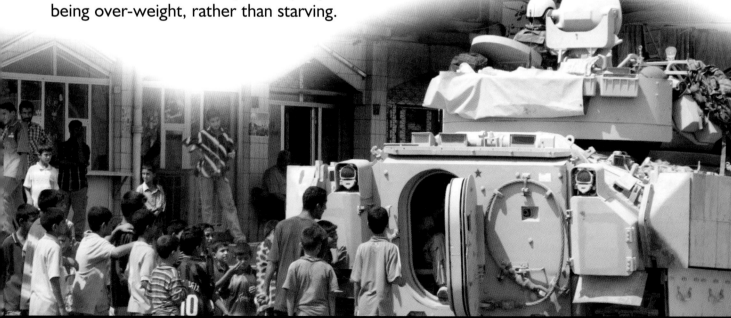

LIFE IN BAGHDAD TODAY: TWO CONTRASTING STORIES

DINA

"My name is Dina. I am nine years old. I wake up at seven o'clock. I wash, dress and eat breakfast.

School starts at eight o'clock. I have many lessons – mathematics, Arabic, geography, drawing, history, sports. Each lesson is 45 minutes long.

Sometimes my mother makes me a sandwich and I have this during my break. I play with my friends in the school garden. I go home at one o'clock when school finishes. Then I do my homework.

After my homework I play a little bit. I like to play ball, or do drawing, or sing songs. In the afternoon there are cartoons on television. Sometimes I help with the cleaning. After that I have dinner, watch TV and then go to bed."

 A classroom at a girls' school.

NORHE

"My name is Norhe. I am twelve years old. I used to go to school every day. But now there are many problems in Baghdad, like kidnappings and bombings, so I have to stay at home. I like school and I feel very sad that I can't go.

I spend my time playing and watching television. Sometimes I can't watch because there's no electricity. I miss my friends and sometimes I get bored. And I miss going out.

The only time I can leave the house now is to visit my uncle who lives nearby. Our family used to go for picnics by the river Tigris, but we don't any more because it's too dangerous.

I hope Baghdad will be safer soon so I can go back to school, and go out more again. Because of all the problems, my family is thinking of leaving Iraq."

WOMEN IN IRAQ HAVE TRADITIONALLY HAD MORE FREEDOM *than in other Arab countries like Saudi Arabia, where Islam is the main source of law. Saddam Hussein's regime was mostly secular – religion did not play a large part in setting the rules.*

Based on a 1959 law, women in Iraq generally had equal rights with men, especially in bigger cities like Baghdad. They worked and studied alongside men in many different fields, from medicine to teaching. They were allowed to drive cars. They had a choice about whether or not to wear veils or headscarves.

Women became even more important in society because of the three wars that Iraq fought under Saddam Hussein. Many men died leaving women as head of the household in most families. They could be a strong force in helping to build a new Iraq.

In 2005 one-quarter of seats in parliament were reserved for women. However, their future equality depends on the interpretation of Iraq's new constitution – the rules for how the country will be run. Will it follow civil law or Islamic law? And how will it be put into practice?

Some women believe that Islamic law (also known as Shari'a law) would be the right choice, because Iraq is a Muslim country. They argue, for example, that Shari'a gives them a better chance of marriage. Under Islamic law, husbands can have four wives and must provide for all their families.

Other women say that, to be fair, issues such as marriage, divorce, child custody and inheritance must be dealt with under a non-religious legal system similar to that of Western countries.

Traditional and modern: two Iraqi women use a digital camera in Baghdad.

Baghdad women shop at a well-stocked market stall selling stationery.

Life in Baghdad: a woman's story

"My name is Tamara. I am 33 years old. I wake up at 5.30 in the morning and make breakfast for my husband and child. Sometimes I make my daughter some sandwiches. My husband goes to work by car. He does official work with the government. Since the war, many streets have been closed so sometimes it takes him one or two hours to get there.

I take my child to school – it's near the house. I come back home. Sometimes I stay there alone, cleaning or washing clothes. Sometimes I visit my neighbours to drink coffee and talk about life. We may go to the market to buy vegetables, or someone may come by with a small caravan, selling things.

I come back and begin cooking – soup, rice, vegetables, chicken. I go to collect my child from school. We have lunch and then I wait for my husband to come home. My child does homework, and sometimes I help her. I may work in the garden or read the newspapers.

In the evening we often visit friends or family, or watch TV. In the old days my daughter would go to sleep at seven o'clock but now she stays awake till ten, eleven, twelve.

Everything depends on electricity – to take a shower, to do the washing. We use gas for cooking. We buy this in the market. You can buy many things on the black market.

At night sometimes I hear fighting or shooting. I am afraid when my husband goes to work and my child is at school.

All you can say is goodbye. I don't know if they'll come back."

AFTER YEARS OF DICTATORSHIP UNDER SADDAM HUSSEIN, *Iraqi people have had the chance to decide how their country will be ruled.*

In 2005, they voted in elections to choose their new leaders. They also approved the new rules for governing Iraq – the constitution.

For many Iraqis, freedom to vote has been sweet. Some cried with joy when they were able to go to polling stations for the first time.

US President George W Bush called Iraqi democracy "a model for the Middle East", which would inspire millions across the region to claim their freedom.

But there are deep wounds in Iraqi society, and they will not heal overnight. During its four-year term, the government chosen in 2005 has to confront some complex issues, like security, how to share money between central government and the regions, and how much of a role Islam will play in a new Iraq.

Benefits of freedom: a woman casts her vote in January 2005.

WHAT DO YOU THINK?

In 2005, the USA had by far the most troops and marines in Iraq (138,000), with 8,500 from Britain. One of their jobs was to train new Iraqi security forces to do the job alone. Many Iraqis wanted the foreign soldiers to go, because it was like an occupation. There were also scandals over the way some US and British soldiers had abused Iraqi prisoners. For the troops too, life was difficult and they were in constant danger of attack. Some people argued that the resistance would tail off if the foreign troops left. But there was no firm deadline for them to go, and for the USA and Britain it would be embarrassing to leave Iraq in a state of chaos. What should happen next?

KNOW YOUR FACTS

Changes in Iraq's media show how much more free Iraq has become since the days of Saddam Hussein. On a typical day just two years after his downfall, you would find critical TV news shows reporting on things like lawlessness and corruption. There were soap operas, or comedies that poked fun at the government. Dozens of newspapers splashed bold headlines across their front pages. Irate Iraqis phoned in to radio shows, lamenting anything from high prices to sewage in the street. Under Saddam Hussein, all this would have been unthinkable.

Each main community is represented, but each wants something different. The Shia and the Kurds suffered years of oppression under Saddam Hussein, and want to sweep away reminders of the old regime dominated by Sunni Arabs. But the Sunnis also need to have their voices heard.

If the Sunnis feel bitter and excluded, they may give up on the political process. Insurgent violence – mostly blamed on the Sunnis – could get worse and bring more chaos. This could all lead to the country breaking up, and even to civil war.

So the future seems to depend on which are stronger: the forces holding Iraq together, or the ones ripping it apart.

Saddam in captivity at a secret location, 2005.

3000BCE The ancient kingdoms of Sumer and Akkad, strong military powers, grow up between the rivers Tigris and Euphrates in a land called Mesopotamia, "the land between two rivers".

1792BCE King Hammurabi leads the Babylon dynasty. The earliest-ever law code is established.

1400BCE The rise of the Assyrian Empire, which takes control of 40 nations and founds great cities like Arbil, Nineveh and Nimrud.

605BCE Revival of the Babylonians under the reign of King Nebuchadnezzar. Civilisation advances with grand building projects like the Hanging Gardens of Babylon.

538BCE Babylon falls to the Persians. Mesopotamia, the "cradle of civilisation" is controlled for the first time by a foreign empire. Domination by foreign powers continues for centuries.

331BCE The Greeks, led by Alexander the Great, take over Mesopotamia and Persia.

126BCE-CE227 The Parthian Persians gain control of the region. They in turn are replaced by a new Persian force, the Sassanian Empire (CE227-636). A struggle for power with the Romans ensues.

CE570 The Prophet Muhammad is born in Mecca. Islam soon stands beside Judaism and Christianity in the number of followers it has.

CE632 The Prophet Muhammad dies in Medina.

CE661-750 His successor, the second caliph, takes power in Mesopotamia. The Muslim Empire spreads far and wide.

CE750-1258 A golden age for Islam. The Abbasid caliphs rule from Baghdad, the new capital of the Muslim Empire. Big steps forward in art, science and literature.

1258-1356 Mongol invaders, commanded by the grandson of Genghis Khan, commit murder and pillage in Baghdad. Arabs become nomadic again.

1356-1534 A succession of rulers: Jalairid dynasty, Turcoman and Safawid Persians all take charge.

1534-1918 The Ottoman Empire: most of modern-day Iraq is conquered by Turkish rulers. They divide Iraq into three provinces – Baghdad, Mosul and Basra.

1920 After Turkey aligns itself with Germany, the losing side in World War One, Iraq comes under British control.

1932 The League of Nations welcomes Iraq as an independent state. It is led by a king chosen by Britain.

1958 The monarchy is overthrown in a military coup, or uprising.

1963 Saddam Hussein's Ba'ath party wins control of Iraq in another coup, then loses it again.

1968 Ba'athists take back control and rule for 35 years without a break.

1979 Saddam Hussein becomes President of Iraq, after running day-to-day affairs for most of the previous decade.

1980-88 Iran-Iraq War. Up to a million people die.

1990 Invasion of Kuwait. Iraqi troops are crushed by international forces, leaving 100,000 dead and 300,000 injured.

2003 A US-led joint force topples Saddam Hussein. Foreign troops occupy Iraq.

2005 Iraqis vote for their new political leaders, and decide on the country's new constitution.

BASIC FACTS

LOCATION: Middle East, between Iran and Kuwait.

TOTAL LAND AREA: 437,072 sq km.

CLIMATE: Two seasons, hot and cool. Iraq often has dust storms, sandstorms or floods.

POPULATION: 26 million (2005 estimate).

AVERAGE AGE: 19 years.

LANGUAGES: Arabic, Kurdish (the official language in the north), Assyrian and Armenian.

CURRENCY: New Iraqi dinar (NID).

LITERACY RATE: 56 per cent of men over 15 can read and write, 24 per cent of women (2003 estimate).

RELIGIONS: Muslim 97 per cent (Shia 60-65 per cent, Sunni 32-37 per cent), Christian or other 3 per cent.

ETHNIC GROUPS: Arab 75-80 per cent, Kurdish 15-20 per cent, Turkoman, Assyrian or other 5 per cent.

INDUSTRIES: Petroleum, chemicals, building materials, fertiliser and food processing.

AGRICULTURE: Dates, rice, wheat, barley, vegetables, cotton, cattle, sheep and poultry. About 50 per cent of the land is arable, but only about 13 per cent is being farmed.

LABOUR FORCE/UNEMPLOYMENT: 6.7 million/ 25-30 per cent of the population (2004 estimate).

TRANSPORTATION: 2,200 km of railways, 45,550 km of highways, 5,275 km of waterways and 111 airports (unknown number damaged during 2003 war).

Arab The original inhabitants of the Arabian Peninsula. A group of people who share language, culture and history.

Autonomy Self-rule. If a place is autonomous, it is semi-independent, with some rights to govern its own affairs.

Caliph A Muslim leader. The Caliphs were the successors to the Prophet Muhammad as leaders of the Muslims.

Constitution The basic rules and agreements on how to run a country.

Coup The toppling of a government or monarch by force.

Democracy A government that has been elected by the people, as opposed to a dictatorship or absolute monarchy.

Dictatorship Absolute rule, using tyranny and oppression.

Ecosystem The natural balance of the environment.

Empire A big collection of states or countries ruled by one single power.

Ethnic-cleansing When a government orders that all people of a particular race living in a specific area be killed or chased from their homes.

Exports Goods sent to another country for sale.

Infrastructure The systems that hold a country together, such as transport and communications.

Mesopotamia An ancient kingdom that existed between the Euphrates and Tigris rivers.

Nomadic To live a wandering life, roaming from place to place in search of grazing land for animals.

Oppression Cruel and brutal treatment, often combined with the denial of human rights.

Ottoman A Muslim Empire, based in what is now Turkey, that was very powerful in the Middle East until the end of World War One.

Revenue Money that comes in from selling something.

Sanctions An economic tool for persuading a country to change its ways, e.g. by not allowing it to trade with other nations.

Secular Not religious.

Shari'a A collection of laws based on the Islamic sacred text, the Koran.

Shia, Shi'ism A minority branch of Islam. The Shia believe that a member of the Prophet Muhammad's direct family should have taken over, when he died in the 7th century.

Sunni A majority branch of Islam, which supported a close friend of the Prophet Muhammad as his successor when he died, rather than a family member. Sunnis take their name from *sunna* meaning "the true path".

USEFUL WEBSITES

http://www.cia.gov/cia/publications/ factbook/geos/iz.html

The CIA World Factbook

http://en.wikipedia.org/wiki/Iraq

A free online encyclopaedia

http://news.bbc.co.uk/cbbcnews/hi/ specials/iraq/default.stm

BBC Newsround special on Iraq

www.bbc.co.uk/iraq and **www.guardian.co.uk/Iraq**

These contain comprehensive coverage of Iraq for older readers.

http://www.iraqigovernment.org/ index_en.htm

Iraqi government official site

www.iraqanalysis.org/

Assessment of post-war Iraq

http://www.al-bab.com/arab/countries/iraq.htm

"Arab Gateway" site: good resources.

http://www.brookings.edu/iraqindex

Resources from independent American thinktank.

http://www.iq.undp.org/

United Nations Development Programme's Iraq project

http://www.unicef.org/emerg/iraq/

UN children's charity on Iraq

Note to parents and teachers:
Every effort has been made by the Publishers to ensure that the websites in this book are suitable for children, that they are of the highest educational value, and that they contain no inappropriate or offensive material. However, because of the nature of the Internet, it is impossible to guarantee that the contents of these sites will not be altered. We strongly advise that Internet access is supervised by a responsible adult.

A

Al-Qaeda 19, 20

Arab 5, 10, 11, 12, 16, 17, 18, 24, 26, 28, 29, 30
Marsh 9

B

Ba'ath party 7, 12, 13, 28, 29

Baghdad 4, 5, 7, 11, 19,-25, 28

Bombings 9, 11, 12, 20, 23

Britain 7, 13, 15, 18, 19, 26, 28

Bush, G W 19, 26

E

Euphrates river 4, 6, 9, 28, 30

F

farming 4, 5, 6, 29

H

Halabjah (gas attack on) 10

Hussein, S 5, 7-13, 15-20, 22, 24, 26-29

I

Iran 4, 7, 10, 16-17, 24, 29

Iraq

children 18, 22-23

coups 7, 12, 13, 28, 30

economy 4, 5, 14, 15

history of 6-7, 28, 29

geography of 4-5, 29

invasion by US 5, 7, 12, 13, 19, 21, 29

invasion of Kuwait 13, 15, 18, 29

peoples 5, 8-11

reconstruction 5, 9, 19, 20, 21, 26, 27

wars 9, 10, 16-19

women 24-25

Islam 5, 6, 7, 8, 24, 28, 30

Shia and Sunni see

separate entries

K

Khomeini, Ayatollah 16

kidnappings 11, 12, 20, 23

Kurdistan 11

Kurds 5, 10-11, 26

Kuwait 4, 13, 14, 15, 18, 29

M

Mesopotamia 6-7, 28, 30

Mongol Empire 7, 28

Muhammad, Prophet 7, 8, 16, 28, 30

O

oil (industry) 4, 5, 11, 13, 14-15, 17, 18

Operation Iraqi Freedom 19

Ottoman Empire 7, 28, 30

P

Persia 7, 16, 28

S

Saudi Arabia 4, 14, 16, 24

Shari'a (law) 24, 30

Shia (Muslims) 5, 8-9, 10, 16, 26, 29, 30

Sunni (Muslims) 5, 8-9, 10, 20, 26, 27, 29, 30

T

Tigris river 4, 6, 9, 12, 23, 28, 30

U

United Nations 18, 19, 22, 31
sanctions 15, 18, 22

USA 9, 10, 13, 15-19, 21, 22, 26, 29
invasion of Iraq 5, 7, 12, 13, 19, 21, 29

W

War, First Gulf 9, 10, 29
Iran-Iraq 10, 13, 15-18, 29

weapons of mass destruction (WMD) 19

World War One 7, 28, 30